My Daily Walk

Finding My Place in the Soul of the Universe

A Collection of Poems
Rebekah Timms

Blue Haven Books

My Daily Walk

Copyright © 2018 Rebekah Timms
Cover design by Rebekah Timms

All rights reserved

ISBN: 978-0-692-11590-9

Published by Blue Haven Books
Printed by IngramSpark

For my sons

Anthony
David
Bradley
Christopher

Acknowledgements

My dear friend Mary Bobo has been with me all the way on this project. She read and edited the drafts and revisions of most of these poems. I am grateful for her steadfast, enthusiastic support and encouragement. My gratitude also extends to my dear friend Dr. Frederick W. Bassett—scholar, poet, novelist—for his faithful support.

CONTENTS

My Daily Walk	11
Just Before Dawn	12
Morning Sounds	13
Who Can Catch a Poet's Dreams?	14
Finding my Way Home	15
My Cat and I	16
My Heart Was Broken But I Didn't Cry	18
Before I Was a Mom	20
Mountain Top Experiences of a Carolina Girl	21
Alone Together	24
The Impetuous Spirit	25
Autumn Leaves	26
Put Your Clothes on for Goodness' Sake	27
My Savannah Townhouse	28
My Latest Love	30
Uneventful Walk	31
Bliss	32
Lucky Me	33
Symphony of the Seasons	34
Guilt	34
The Good Life	35
Being Alive	36
Revitalization (The House Across the Street)	38
Reflections of the Spirit	40
Life Cycles	41
Thou Shalt Not Covet	42
Footsteps on the Other Side of the World	43

CONTENTS (continued)

Michael	44
How Love Sounds	46
A New Season	47
Blathering Platitudes	48
Mask Charade	49
Moonlight Sonata	50
Wren's Nest	51
Reality Check	52
Two for the Price of One	54
Dilemma or Delight	55
Friends	56
A True Friend	57
Captivity	58
Capricorn	59
The Life of a Dreamer	60
Silhouettes	62
A Day at the Beach	63
What is Beauty?	64
Spaces in My Life	66
The Winters of Life	67
Contentment	68
Funeral in My Home Town	70
Free Walking	72
When to Get Off the Codger-Crowded Dance Floor	73
Don't Forget to Look in the Mirror	74
When the Novelty Wore Off	76
The Eyes Have It	77

CONTENTS (continued)

Connections	78
Umbrellas	79
Old Woman and Cat	80
Annual Christmas Party	81
My Trusting Heart	82
I Want to Go Back	83

My Daily Walk

A Collection of Poems

"I love cats because I enjoy my home and little by little they become its visible soul."
—*Jean Cocteau (1889-1963)*

My Daily Walk

As I round a certain bend in the road
sometimes a gentle wind greets
and then overtakes me....
my step quickens, becomes effortless,
like that of a magnificent horse....
not a beautiful racehorse, but an old mare
who has been released from the gravity
which heretofore slowed her pace
and gradually ravaged her body
and today has allowed her to soar into
the cadence of a perfectly executed trot.
My mane blows in the wind
and my chin is lifted high.
I am peaceful and happy. All is well.

Tomorrow may not be the same.
Sometimes that gentle wind
does not greet me,
or perhaps I do not notice it.
But every now and then, it does, and
I glide across an open plain, unrestricted.
Then the gentle wind releases me,
and my footsteps touch the good earth.
I am myself again.

Just Before Dawn

The morning chill pushes the purity
and freshness of dawn into my pores.
I walk toward the east, awaiting the
fragile moment just before the sun
presents beyond the horizon,
before the heavy breath of
downtrodden mankind filters out the
warmth and promise of light.
The magnificent light. If we could
just seek to bask in it, instead of
lurking behind in the darkness, and
dare to become the goodness we hold
deep inside. The monotonous drone
of life greets the morning sun as
people shuffle to their noisy cars and
sag beneath the dark shadows that
beset them, shadows of their own
making, unaware of the clarity and
newness of the unsullied dawn.

Morning Sounds

My thumping footsteps down the hall
the splashing water in the sink
the gurgling of the coffee pot
prompt me to pause and think

about the pleasant morning sounds
greeting the silent break of dawn.
My own chuckle I barely hear,
as I watch my Kitty yawn.

The rustling of the morning paper
and creaking of my old oaken chair
are the comforting sounds of sameness
that make each day seem rare.

Door blinds rattle as I step out
to catch the familiar morning view
and find I'm like a stranger there—
things look so fresh and new.

Who Can Catch the Poet's Dreams?

They are flung into the air and
penetrate our skin like sea mist.
Words are scattered all about us
and enter our souls,
soothing the restless heart.
They push into our ears
and plunge us into our own
mysterious thoughts,
helping us understand
who and why we are.

Finding My Way Home

The building could be a stately college
campus library or a city courthouse
with dark paneling boasting its patina
and rich heritage. The large room
I have entered from a side entrance
is void of people, and I struggle to open
the massive double doors to escape.

The scaffolding has scant flooring
supported by a maze of bars and crossbars
painted orange. Atop this structure I fight
my way through turbulent wind, toward
a window on the top floor of the building
it surrounds. Time and its relevance
are unknown factors.

The midafternoon sun shines on a familiar
six-lane boulevard, with missing traffic
lights and signage. Instinct warns me
that deception is afoot.
If only I could remember.

Recurring dreams of being lost take me
to these settings over and over. What
does my wandering soul want me to
find there? What did I leave along
the way that my heart yearns to retrieve?

My Cat and I

Both of us have forgotten what
used to rub us the wrong way.

We know we are supposed
to act uppity and perturbed
every now and then, when things
annoy us.

We just aren't easily annoyed
anymore.

Now we don't even rush
through a door as soon as it opens
or feel obligated to eat everything
in our bowls.

The rasping noises and high-pitched
voices of life do little to disturb our
repose; although in response
we might stretch a bit
or roll our weight to the other side.

These shifts in our psyches
have not rendered us nonplussed
but have produced in us
a sage and stately mindset
that assures us of our maturity.

How peaceful we are, my cat and I.

"The ideal calm exists in a sitting cat."
—Jules Reynard (1864-1910)

My Heart Was Broken But I Didn't Cry

My playmate's mother was generous when she handed me an umbrella and closed the door. It was suppertime, never mind that the rain was blowing right into my face and the trip home was on a slight incline. Under my free arm I wedged a thin paper bag which held my beloved paper dolls. These, along with my bride doll, were my favorite possessions.

Obedient child that I was, I walked close to the curb on the street, where of course a small river was forming. The wind lifted the umbrella a bit. As I struggled to hold on to it, the paper bag slid out from under my arm and dispersed some of its contents into the flooding waters. I can still feel the rain on my back as I gathered up what remained of my treasures and made my way home, only a few houses up the street but today a daunting trek.

Inside Mother helped me spread all the paper dolls, dresses and accessories on the enamel and chrome kitchen table to dry. We didn't talk about the misfortune. We didn't discuss how the situation might have been averted. We smiled when most of the paper items dried out crisp and barely wrinkled. I brushed the hopeless casualties into the dust pan and sat down to a cup of hot chocolate. This is the way Mother and I handled life's little inconveniences.

Before I Was a Mom

I never knew the pleasant feel of a little
boy's sandy hand being slipped
into mine as we strolled down the beach
gathering seashells…

Or in the midst of the tightest hug
a little boy could give, felt the heartbeat
of one who thought I was
the greatest Mom on earth…

Or sat in the audience on graduation
day and watched my confident
little boy slip into manhood…

Or choked on the happy emptiness
of seeing my son look into the face
of his new bride…

I wouldn't have missed it for the world.

Mountain Top Experiences of a Carolina Girl

Born and raised near the foothills of the Blue Ridge Mountains, I think I was drawn into the lore and the lure of the hills with my first step. Claiming his Scots-Irish, Appalachian heritage my grandfather sang old Irish folk songs to me when I was too young to ask the questions that presented themselves later when I listened to his clear tenor voice rendering his quaint, melodic stories and grabbing the attention of my young son.

I remember my childhood experience of gazing into the vastness before me as I stood with my mother at Caesar's Head, the outcropping atop the Blue Ridge Escarpment. I expected to hear the deep, rich sound that I imagined should accompany the spectacle and fill the space. But silence prevailed, and I was forced to begin playfully pulling mother's hand, urging her closer to the edge and hoping she would not comply.

During my teenage years the mountains meant going to Oconee State Park Summer JHA Camp and vying for the attention of the handsome, blond and tanned boy who was our activities director and taught us how to square dance. Late one summer I received an exquisitely crafted cedar jewelry box and an Indian turquoise ring, gifts my boyfriend brought to me from Highlands, which I perceived to be a remote mountain location where arcane, mute, native Indians created their wares.

Later I visited the Smoky Mountains with my oldest son, wife and two children. We pitched tents by the Pigeon River and fried breakfast bacon on a Coleman stove. Our wilderness experience was not in the least diminished by the fact that our campsite was squeezed in with those of other, I assume, happy, eager families. Strangely I hardly noticed them, until with gratitude I watched one of them jump in the water to help my son reconnect with his daughter, after her safety tether slipped through his fingers while they were tubing down the river.

A few years ago, same son and family sat with me on top of Big Bald Mountain at Wolf Laurel at the Appalachian trailhead. He had just hiked a portion of the trail and his face beamed satisfaction. Just before sunset we gathered our things and quietly, almost reverently, made our way down the trail to our rented mountain house. My son has grandchildren now. Maybe he will take them to this special place someday. I don't suppose I'll be going.

Out west I ascended a mountain in the Harquahala Range in Arizona with my youngest son. We climbed into his Dodge Ram truck and headed for the peak. With a CD of banjo music plugged in we bounced along a rugged, treacherous dirt road, truck engine roaring, windows down, my occasional squeals blending in with our laughter, and all leaving in the wake of dust behind us a stream of strange music. At the top of the mountain were the remains of a 1920 solar observatory. Here the mysterious sounds created by the relentless rush of the wind around us overtook our conversation and sensibilities. We were left to gaze at the beauty in pleasurable isolation.

With my children, their children I have listened to the splashing waters of the Pigeon River in the Smokies, experienced the push of the wind atop the Harquhala Mountains in Arizona, and felt the vibrations of eternity as we sat at the trailhead of the Appalachian Trail on Bald Mountain. These and other mountain memories quicken my senses and evoke the sounds of my childhood imagination.

Alone Together

Yes, it is an oxymoron
But I love using one when
I want to grab someone's
Attention and enjoy
Watching the lightbulb
Go off and the
Smug expression
Ooze across the faces
Of those who not only
Get it
But are attracted to it
Because they themselves
As I
Are contradictions.

The Impetuous Spirit

The impetuous spirit sways above the hushed din of the circumspect, plodding through their lives beneath her. She flaunts her laughter and observes their pursed lips as they keep their cards close to the vest.

The impetuous spirit is never lonely, nor does she care to intrude upon those who are. The winds of change blow past her like a flock of seagulls, and she ignores their tell-tale caws that sound the warning of the dark clouds forming on the horizon.

The impetuous spirit shakes off the cloak of regret and unanswered questions and embraces the warmth of the flowing robe of confidence and unconquerable pride. She rebuffs the melancholy that slowly impinges upon the pace of the music and the dance.

The impetuous spirit never changes; she simply adjusts to the narrowed scope of existence which accompanies her diminishing presence and relevance in life. She swirls and preens in her dreams and hardly notices that her envious admirers have long since abandoned her.

Autumn Leaves

A small clearing at the edge of the forest invites me to enter the vibrant spectacle of autumn. The trees brandish their color like a dancer's scarf. I move among them, stretching tall and raising my arms in celebration of the season.

What am I to make of the nostalgia that overcomes me as I watch leaves swirl gently to the ground? My path is covered with a visual cacophony of colorful symbols of renewal, one by one validating the eternal rhythms of the earth. What beckons me to acknowledge the beauty of each leaf as it finds its resting place?

Looking up at my companions, I am called to take part in their ritual. I breathe in their earthy smells and long to revive passions of life grown brittle with time and to exhale my harbored, withered dreams. The warmth of expectancy creates fresh sensations within me.

The angled rays of the sun shed new light on the fallen leaves. They become my foibles, my wasted intentions, destined to dwindle beneath the winter snows, to be ever washed away by the spring rains.

Put Your Clothes On, For Goodness' Sake

I've been around a while, and I've known a few emperors in my lifetime. You have, too. Sitting on our mothers' laps we met our first one. In wide-eyed amazement we looked down on the pages of our fairy tale books and watched a naked man, the Emperor no less, parade through the streets. Most likely, we were less puzzled by the emperor's behavior than that of the spectators.

I wish I could remember when I identified the next emperor in my life, with or without his courtiers and subjects. By the time I did recognize him I had probably filtered many observations of my fellow man through the life lessons gained from my first encounter with Hans Christian Andersen's emperor. Oh, and I've met the clever weavers and the fawning crowds. What childhood dismisses as frivolity, sage minions of the adult world embrace. People go on draping themselves with illusions while those around them complacently allow the parade to continue. Strike up the band!

My Savannah Townhouse

The house was purchased in April 1979. My youngest son had celebrated his ninth birthday in March. With my little boys growing more self-sufficient by the day, there was time for me, and the inclination, to take on a personal adventure. Looking back on this time in my life I uncovered an amazing truth, which is that one's life can be beautifully enriched and influenced by surrounding oneself with new friends. I tend to cling steadfastly to old ones, but moving from city to city necessitates putting old friends in storage sometimes. Several of my new friends in Decatur, Alabama owned similar houses.

I was in love with the house as soon as I laid eyes on it. The sales contract allowed me to make monthly deposits toward a down payment until the house was finally mine. Every furnishing item placed in this house was carefully selected from specialty shops, antique stores, catalogues and two from the Smithsonian Institute Gift Shop.
I repurposed some personal items as well.
The house was perfect.

When I moved to St. Louis the house stayed closed up and unused for a while. Moving back to Greenwood, SC was the occasion for a grand re-opening, after which my granddaughter, Lauren, and I thoroughly revived and enjoyed my treasure. So much so, that by the turn of the century there was a complete refurbishing of the house: new wiring, fixtures, carpet and accessories. I brought a young lady from England home with me to live in the house. I'll never forget seeing her standing in the house for the first time.

Alas, tragedy struck in the form of three waves of grandchildren about ten years apart. The first casualty was a dislodging of the wiring system caused by my young grandson chasing son Brad's two uninvited cats right under the foundation of the house. Then came the persistent rearranging and breakage of household items by the next granddaughter. With the arrival of more grandsons came the unhinging of the front door and the destruction of the newel post and delicate banisters of the front stairs. Another amazing truth uncovered: under-supervised grandchildren can be dangerous.

I finally had the entire house moved from the dining room to the lesser accessible master bedroom down the hall. Some restoration has occurred, but my dollhouse has somehow lost a bit of her dignity. The wear and tear of a peopled life, no matter how beloved, takes its toll on one.

MY LATEST LOVE

Quite a specimen, he is! Thick hair,
stately demeanor. He was brought to
my front door and introduced to me
by someone who thought we would
be a good match.

And she was right, as soon as he got over
the sting of being ousted by the woman
he had been living with for several years.

The greatest thing we have going
is our desire, to maintain our own space,
that is. I once followed him down to
the pond, where he sat looking out over
the water. He was annoyed and playfully
hid from me! I liked that.

We are alike in many ways, both prone
to impulsive, eccentric behavior.
We easily forget each other's mistakes.
We love cuddling by the fire.

Ah, my latest love, my all-time favorite
is growing old. He is fifteen already.
He has been the best cat I ever had.

An Uneventful Walk

Not much to think about today as I walked.
Then I saw the heron gazing into the pond
from which comes sustenance.
A turtle popped up from the water and
climbed onto a rock for no particular reason
but to sun and enjoy life.
And across the way a watchful mother goose
stretched her head above the trusting
brood clustered about her…

"All I have needed Thy
hand hath provided. Great
is Thy faithfulness."

Bliss

Ah, the sweet simplicity of life and love
which too many of us are missing.
Some just don't get it.
Late in the evening when I look in the mirror
after brushing my teeth and see that my hair has
not been combed all day, I wonder not that
the hair remains uncombed, but why it is so
disheveled. Then I chuckle at how much time and
effort I spent today crawling around on my hands
and knees and reaching into dark places in an
attempt to rescue the chipmunk which my beloved
cat, who is obsessed with the hunt, laid at my feet
in the living room. The chipmunk, rattled but
unscathed, escaped out the opened deck door,
while my bemused cat stoically washed his face.
Later, hoping to match my cat's productivity
I scattered a few words across a page in my
journal. What an easy day. Clad in last night's
pajamas, I turn off the light and slip into bed.
How convenient I forgot to dress today.

Lucky Me

Lucky me, the message read,
followed by pictures
of mountain skylines,
Joshua trees, a lone tent sitting
near a patch of saguaro cacti,
and majestic desert rock
formations.
All from the heart of my son,
Chris, an earthly soul
who moves through life
like the wind and rain,
swirling and washing
over the beauty of nature.
Wherever he goes, he belongs.
He hears the sounds,
smells the scents,
and senses the strength that
bolsters the earth and
divides its deepest canyons.
With the stealth of a young
Indian brave, he explores
the forest, steers his canoe
over the waters
and passionately reveres
his surroundings.
His presence is timeless.

Symphony of the Seasons

The pulsing early spring buds murmur
the sound of musicians tuning their instruments.
Lush summer flowers burst forth into the familiar,
playful or grand overture we anticipate.
A crescendo of fall color creates the autumn event;
the symphony begins. Winter snow on the
pinecones ushers in the quiet music of advent.
Then the glorious finale: Christmas is here!

Guilt

Racism! Confederate Flag! Plight of the
Native Americans! People running around
looking for excuses for being who they are,
fearful of who they might become. Enough!
Move forward. Cease the lumbering along
in search of a cause. What is life but a flight
from our own demons? Not a struggle with
history or circumstances, but a struggle with
one's own psyche.

> **Variety may be the spice of life,
> but it is sameness, constants and
> tradition that bring me comfort.**

The Good Life

Would that she could have recaptured
the cherished dreams that once swirled around
her frame and eddied her right off the sands
and into the blue skies of the Carolina beaches.
Did not those very dreams push her through gates
and over hurdles until they became reality?
Did she not pursue them with all the vigor of
youthful expectation?

It was the good life, until she found herself
teetering on the rim of adventure, guided,
or misguided, by the anticipated rush
of freefall. Thus she plunged, relying on the
Safety Net to catch which one of her fell
into it. Rescued and grateful for the rebound,
she scrambled off the net. A familiar, blithely
naïve smile crossed her face. The Carolina girl
squeezed herself back into the good life, not yet
fully equipped to resist the exhilarating
pull of impulse or the desire to take flight
on the wings of a distant dream.

Being Alive

To me, there is nothing in this world more dramatic than the rising and setting of our sun. Consider it. We earthly beings know and feel and are tugged deep in our souls by the order of the universe. Does the sun sink one second before its appointed time into the nameless color of the western sky? Nameless because human conception of pink or coral can scarce describe its beauty. Do the weary bones of the gatherer compel the sun to hasten its repose so he might lay down his hoe a moment earlier?

Creation responds to the creator. Does an acorn resent that a blade of grass is trying to displace it? Does a field of flowers mourn when the heavy foot of the gardener shortens the life of one of them? Does a sheep resist the shearer who is relieving it of a heavy burden? Does a happy kitten question the morning sun that pours through the window and warms him?

With the knowledge that we are part of God's magnificent universe, is it possible that we fret and bemoan our plight on this earth? Does not the overwhelming joy of being alive soften our earthly suffering, impelling us to cling to the simplicity of a happy memory or a pleasant day? We are here, we are one, we belong,
we are the universe, we cannot be erased.

"The smallest feline is a masterpiece"
—Leonardo Da Vinci (1452-1519)

Revitalization
The House Across the Street

The house across the street from me has been
empty for a while.

Now she is being renovated, and I noticed this
morning how proud she looks. The tips of the
sharp angles of her roofline appear higher, and
she is losing the sagging look that sometimes
drapes itself over a vacant house.

Layers of neglect have been scraped off her inner
being and are being carried out the back door.
Her sullied carpet has been yanked off the floor
and lies on the front lawn for all to observe,
yet destined to oblivion in a distant landfill,
like the faded memories of the fine lady
who once dwelt within her walls.

The house across the street from me is now
different from what it was because of the life
which is pushing through her doors and windows
on all sides and rushing into her
as she breathes in the beauty of it.

I look forward to a late evening soon when I will
see lights in her windows, flowers on her porch
and vibrance in her soul. Emptied now filled,
wilted now revived, silent now pulsating,
she will step forward and resume her place
in God's universe.

Welcome, I will smile, as I hope for a March wind
that will cast away the last clinging cobweb from
my frame and remove the brittle, dead leaves
that clog my gutters. I will stand tall and allow
the spring rain to wash the film from my windows
for a clearer inward and outward view.
I will cherish the one that dwells in me.

Reflections of the Spirit

Crossroads, failures, imperfections.
I seem to be very forgiving of myself.
Where is my guilt? Where are my tears?
My happiness and peace of mind come easily,
partly I think, because of my mother, who
without a word and with her very presence,
made me feel valid and worthy.

We must seek healing, I am told. From what?
I could list the tragedies in my life, some
very tangible, some electric, some pitiable.
I have already dealt with the wounds;
it is as though they never existed.
Why is this? What have I done with the sorrow?
I am not listening for an answer.

When the skeleton of my soul starts to bend,
God emerges as the strength of my existence. My
present need is resilience against the lost hope of
perfect lives for my sons. Motherhood overwhelms
me only when I see traces of life's challenges on
the faces of my sons and cannot will them away.

Life Cycles

Four stately old oak trees shade my home from the relentless summer sun. In late autumn their leaves create a swath of color against a bright blue sky. In time the leaves are scattered across my lawn and tossed inadvertently into the air to settle in bothersome clumps on my gable pitched roof. The activity appears hurried and utile. Raking the leaves becomes my role in the drama of the sustaining earth rhythms.

Beneath the leafless limbs of the trees, my windows and rooftop are laid bare to receive the warmth of the winter sun. On my deck I sit comforted by the elegant oaks, standing strong and beautiful without adornment.

After spring thunderstorms, I do not resent picking up after my benefactors. I enjoy early morning strolls around the yard, gathering twigs and branches, lugging them to the roadside for pickup, getting rid of the deadwood. When summer arrives, my oak trees and I will be unencumbered by last year's decay. Perhaps the clutter we have dispersed will bring enrichment to a distant soil.

Thou Shalt Not Covet

The purse is a tapestry of rich color,
texture and whimsy. A mélange of
deep burgundy, green, beige and gold
ribbons, beads and fanciful metal
embellishments. Oh, how I wanted
this beautiful purse. One Sunday
morning at church as I caressed the
twinkling, beaded fringe on the purse,
I asked its owner, my dear friend
Mildred, to bequeath it to me and to
my delight she said she would.
Several years later, a few days before
Christmas, Mildred paid me a visit.
As we sat on my sofa chatting over
a glass of wine, she handed me
a beautifully wrapped gift. Being one
who adores receiving surprise gifts,
I opened it immediately. There was
the purse, its beauty eclipsed only by
that of the smile on my friend's face.
"I wanted you to enjoy it now,"
she said. I treasure my lovely purse
and the genuine friendship it represents.
Thou shalt not covet?

Footsteps on the Other Side of the World

Walking the level terrain of my neighborhood,
slightly more than fifteen miles from where I was
born, I am reminded of the evenness of my life
in its waning years. Oh, along the way I have met
hills and valleys of my own making. Ill winds have
blown against me and pushed me to the brink of a
cliff, more than once, where from out of the chasm
I was met with the rush of a greater counterforce.

This morning halfway 'round the world my
youngest son stretches his strong, slender legs
and mounts the Balkans of Bulgaria,
pausing now and then to gather the grandeur
of God's canyons and gorges. He sends pictures
to me, and I sense that he is blended into the scene
and the universe he loves. My footsteps are steady
on the ground beneath me, but my spirit is
transported to a place in Bulgaria, where it drifts
along with my son, claiming his adventure,
experiencing the beauty of his heart and soul.

Michael

My eyes were misty when I looked back at Mother on her front porch, gracefully moving her hand back and forth in one last motion of sadness that our visit was over. As we pulled onto the highway I looked over my shoulder to return her wave and once more lock the familiar scene into my bittersweet-memory file. Sometimes I open that file and clearly see her beautiful face.

Then I see my nephew Michael running across the yard lifting a thermos of coffee high into the air like a victory torch and yielding the potion that would keep us alert, bear us safely home to St. Louis! His lank six-feet-four-inch frame glides across the grass, his bright smile barely shines through his ample beard and mustache. We turn back to accept his offering.

Michael went out west for a while after that and returned home with a cactus plant he had potted after discreetly plucking it from the desert. The next time I saw him his long legs were folded into position in a wheel chair. For weeks he had fought for his life and for months fought to recover from injuries received in an automobile wreck, which ultimately claimed his mobility but never erased his smile.

The prickly pear cactus plant was passed down to me a few years ago. My gloved and sleeved son Chris lifted it from its bondage and plopped it down into a mound of sand that we borrowed from a sand trap on the golf course. Most of the original plant died, but new pads pushed through the sand and survived. This year bright yellow flowers appeared on Michael's misshapen old cactus reminding me of his unflagging smile.

How Love Sounds

Hearing my Mother's charm bracelet
tinkling was like tiny fairies doing
their happy dance around my head.
Small silver charms dangled from her
bracelet, one for each grandchild,
and they made such pleasant noises
against each other when Mother was
busy. She was always busy, helping
me fold endless stacks of laundry,
hemming a new dress she had made
for me, kneading dough for a batch
of cheese biscuits, creating exquisite
Christmas tree ornaments. When her
visits were over, I strained to hear
the jingle of her bracelet as she waved
goodbye to us at the airport. Every
graceful gesture Mother made was
full of love and her tinkling bracelet
scattered it all around us.

A New Season

The summer days are shortening;
the air is still hot, but it carries the sense of change.

As I walked today I noticed
that the mother goose no longer stands taller
than her brood but appears taller as she
stands above them on the bank of the pond.
She started to make her way
toward the pond, and the small crowd parted
to allow her passage.
She slipped into the water, and as she moved
smoothly toward the center of the pond
the brood was watching her.
Once she seemed to be looking back at them.
There was movement among the group.
They glanced at one another, but none
followed her.

The mother goose alone on the water looked
so peaceful and serene. I imagined her to be
quite proud of her grownup goslings.
I even think she was smiling.

Blathering Platitudes

Famous quotations no longer spoken with candor: *Something good will come out of this. That which does not kill us makes us stronger. When one door closes, another opens.*

Groan and roll your eyes, if you will.
Then go back to the beginning of your story. Revisit the plateau in your life that launched you into a new adventure. Examine the shining moments of your experience and perhaps reveal unrecognized, preceding darkness. Seek out the impetus of your periods of heightened creativity.

They are all in there, these trite old bromides, twisting in and out of our tales of survival. I am not embarrassed by them – but I won't be interjecting them into serious conversations with my sophisticated, intelligent friends.
Let alone my sons.

Mask Charade

The freedom of well-nurtured children surely transcends any other human experience. Even in the midst of shadows, these fortunate little creatures find beauty, safety, wonder and laughter at every turn. This magical state settles into their souls and is joyfully revived again and again as they grow up and life grows dull and surprises lack delight.

The first encounter with freedom lost is the unexpected, disruptive adolescent scramble of jumping from simply *being* to trying to understand the illusive persona which has been assigned to him. He overhears a description of himself from the lips of his parents and wants to shout, *Wait, this isn't me!* Maybe the shout is dispatched, but no one hears.

So he chooses a person to emulate, an older sibling, a parent, a special friend or a pop culture figure and joins the masquerade, playfully enslaved behind the masks that hide his true identity. The sudden arrival of adulthood is liberating; the world is his again! The mask of conformity lingers but does not overshadow the young at heart, who being masters of mime, work their guileless magic.

Moonlight Sonata

Come, truth seekers,
be drawn into the allure
of the shimmering cool
of moonbeams.
Pass through the ethereal strings
of Sophia's lyre, a prism
bending and blending the colors
of your soul into the music
of the paisley swirls around you.
Yield to the swelling desire
for the touch of her deft fingers
guiding you
into her mystical reverie.
Be loosed forever into the sublime.

Wren's Nest

The nest was carefully tucked into the
new spring wreath on my front door.
I wondered how long it had been there
when I startled a pair of little wrens,
perhaps putting the final touches on their nest.
They fluttered away early one morning
when I opened the door to get the daily paper.
I doubted they would return after the door
slammed hard as I stepped outside.
Oh please come back, I muttered to myself.
The nest was deep, and I never laid eyes on
the eggs. One day some tiny white down
shimmered in the late afternoon sunshine.
I stopped using the front door and monitored
the activity by approaching the front porch
from my garage. Soon I could distinguish
three little beaks thrust upward, awaiting
their morning meal. All was well.
The chicks grew larger, and the day the nest
was empty I remembered the sad days when
one by one my boys, four of them, flew from
the nest and nurture I had provided.
*Little mother wren, next year you will fill
another nest, but mine is forever empty.*

Reality Check

Reality check? Fie! I am far from pulling out that map, looking for Introspection Avenue. That's for those who stand at the intersection of Maturity Lane and Self Awareness Boulevard. You've been there, exhaling the stale breath of the magnificent quest and inhaling the smug rush of having arrived. This is where, exempt from socio-economic comparisons and paradigms, we built our dream homes and raised our prodigies.
I still sit and listen to the lyrics set to the music of an old Russian folk song. Those were the days, my friend.

I linger at that intersection. I have mourned the loss of old trees that needed to be replaced and pulled out pictures of the original facades of the buildings. I have been around longer than some of them. Always the pragmatist, I have been resilient to change; there was always an alternative side street or a less traveled road to pursue. These paths have narrowed, become less navigable.

The freedoms that buoy the lives of the elderly lose all significance when the tide goes out and carries with it friends, family members, drivers licenses and even sensibility. Ah yes, I will face the reality check. I will take the high road of gratitude and joy, spend time with family and friends and proclaim myself a poet.

Two for the Price of One

Since I have always loved to find bargains, it stands to reason that with one hospital stay and only nine months invested I brought in two priceless little baby boys. The investment strategy had been in the planning and development stage for a period of ten years, but the dividends came pouring in immediately, with daily deposits times two…and then some. Advisory fees were minimal, everyone had an inside tip for me, including the check-out clerk at Target, who suggested I invest in pharmaceuticals, i.e., birth control pills. Advice, yes. Hands on management, *nada*. Our free-loading, vacationing relatives stayed home that year, expecting limited return on investment I suppose. Little did they know that my pair of hedge funds would produce capital gains that even Buffett would envy. My memory bank is worth a fortune, rich with the things that money can't buy, as well as the pride and joy of being the issuer of two of the greatest IPO's ever to hit the market.

Dilemma or Delight

Birds a-hoppin', buds a-poppin'
and here I linger
over a half a cup of cold coffee
celebrating an empty calendar day!
Like an irregular row of ants
choices queue up before me,
vying for my attention.
I name them.
Good Deeds stumbles and gets
shoved to the back of the line.
Thank-you-note breaks down
along with *Pencil Point*.
Fibermop gets lost in the dust.
I stop assigning names to them.
One by one they shuffle off the
edge of my table.
I snatch *Writingpad,* just before
she slips out of reach,
and I warm my cup of coffee.

Friends

Like summer storm clouds
they materialize on the horizon
when least expected and jolt
you with their passion and
tenacity.
They grab your heart and
you grow to understand them
and begin to cling
hungrily to the pleasure
they bring.
Often you do not set out
to gather them, they simply
come to you, and somehow
you know they will stay.
At night you close your
eyes and see them twinkling
like tiny stars in the darkness
of your evening reverie, and
you tremble with gratitude.

A True Friend

Mock not the boastful soul whose good
fortune brings him to expand upon it!
As his chest swells with satisfaction,
draw a deep breath and allow yourself to
experience his grand moment. When the
exuberance deflates into quiet
contemplation, sit with him and reflect
on the memory of his genuine successes.
Laugh with him as he recalls his own
youthful bravado. Like a true friend,
adjust to the tempo as the journey unfolds.

Mock not the boastful soul who has
crowned himself, danced to an unfinished
symphony and now sits with the chagrin
of premature celebration. Be with him as
he shakes the dust off, recovers from his
miscalculations, and treads the tangled
path of reclamation. Require of him no
flimsy explanation. Allow him to ride on
the coattails of your forgetfulness.
Like a true friend, listen to his hopeful
plans for the future and believe in them.

Captivity

At the last second I turn back
to face those wistful eyes
straining to will away
my departure.
I wave my hand. Her head lifts
slightly up from her pillow.

In the hallway
I pass chairs with wheels
propelled by frail hands
and shuffling feet.
I avoid the weary stares
and quicken my step.

Into the summer sunshine
and flowers I burst.
I release a long, purging sigh
and watch the freedom around me.
Automobiles. A squirrel.
A little boy on a skateboard.

Soon I will return home
and find sitting in the window
my declawed, housebound
cat who longs to be outside.

Capricorn

I have been watching a persistent squirrel riding my rodent-proof birdfeeder. His tail is twitching and he is scratching the sides of the inaccessible. Every now and then he jumps off and goes scurrying up the adjacent tree and down again, ending in a wild leap onto the feeder. He then meekly looks around, wondering who or what might be observing his folly.
I am starting to laugh….
I am seeing myself!
Twitching, scratching, scurrying, wildly leaping through life, refusing to give up on futile endeavors, jumping from one sphere of activity to another.
Wait a minute, I am a Capricorn! I have a sense of purpose, great faith in my ability….talk to you later. I have things to do.

The Life of a Dreamer

By the time Daryl was fifteen years old
he had formed a rock band and was booking
gigs in county juke joints and honky-tonks
where patrons would tolerate the new rock
sound and his own compositions. Daryl was
the lead singer and on keyboard, his younger
brother Bruce was on percussion. Their
mother, my sister, bought an old van and
sewed costumes for the five-man group. She
drove them to rural night clubs, where out
of costume the under-aged boys would never
have been allowed entry and where my
sister would not have otherwise been found.

Daryl was a talented musician and created
a collection of playful dance music as well
as haunting melodies, together symbols of
the highs and lows of his life. He attended
Berklee College of Music in Boston and
tried to make a career in music. Instead he
spent his final weeks in Boston alone in an
apartment fighting off cocaine addiction.
He left his rock star dream in the city,
as well as his young wife and tiny blond
curly-haired daughter. He came home clean
and stayed that way. He continued writing
music and lyrics throughout his life.

Daryl moved to Myrtle Beach and to the amazement of the folks back home launched a successful real estate career. He started designing homes, was hired by a developer and made a name for himself in the local industry. He designed and developed his own ground up project. As his financial position was flourishing so was his lifestyle and generosity. A couple of failed ventures and several wives later, Daryl found himself in the midst of another fading dream. Mustering enough financial backing to build a million dollar home in Mount Pleasant, he furnished it and placed it on the market.
It became a stark finale to his life.

Not long after the for-sale sign was hung, Daryl died of complications from cancer. His wake was held in this home. Tearful friends and business associates spoke highly of him. Four of the six women in his life, three wives and three companions, lovingly and with no regret described years of life with the handsome dreamer.
The voices of his children and step-children gave testimony to the cheerful, loyal, generous nature of their father. A stepdaughter wistfully shared, "He taught us the meaning of the word home."

Silhouettes

As I walk, the sun at my back casts
its rays upon the length of my frame,
creating on the smooth pavement
what belongs only to me, my shadow.
I have watched her over the years;
her back is not as straight as it was,
her shoulders a bit rounded.
She is wider. Sometimes I imagine that
I see her swinging a rubber swim cap
on the tips of her fingers, a beach towel
over her arm, tanned legs striding toward
the local swimming pool. Head high,
pace rhythmic. Then I see a little boy
holding her hand, his chin up, eagerly
watching her face as her feet splash
through ripples of a receding ocean wave.
Now her slender body leans forward,
muscles taut as she looks back at
three little boys in the wagon she is
pulling, silhouettes in the late afternoon
sun. We mount the front steps, and my
shadow fades into the shaded corner
of the porch. Closing the door gently,
I smile, wondering what memories we
might conjure up tomorrow.

A Day at the Beach

Under a toadstool
Crept a wee elf
In this case
The elf was myself
The toadstool an umbrella
And myself not so wee
On the beach of Kiawah
As happy as I could be.

What is Beauty?

Somedays even the most ordinary thing
becomes beautiful.

The round tabletop made of cement tiles
of different shades of tan, having lost its base of
wrought iron to rust, is propped against the
banister of my deck, and today
is a work of art.

The pile of leaves and twigs, standing
in testimony to my half-hour or so attempt to tidy
up my back yard, is of itself worthy of a poem.

Resting on a small table, my glass of cabernet
celebrates a beautiful early spring day and is
radiant with the late afternoon sun
highlighting the richness of its color.

The memory of the character I saw chiseled
in the face of a friend who sat beside me
in church this morning
is a portrait of steadfast human spirit.

Beauty is the ability to see and enjoy and
treasure our moments in time.

Beauty is that it doesn't matter that my table
is broken or that the leaves and twigs are
brittle and dead or that the glass of wine has
been imbibed and replaced by another
or that my friend and I may not share
the same pew in church next Sunday.

Somedays all things are beautiful.

Spaces in My Life

An empty, cloth-lined wicker basket sits on the top shelf of my Christmas decorations closet, standing ready to accommodate new joys and mysterious acquisitions...store them until they lose their luster and trickle down, one by one to the bottom shelf, allowing the process to begin anew. The shelves in this closet are quite tidy, except for the bottom one where everything is jumbled up, like the crowded places in my heart where
laughter mingles with tears until both inseparably blend into one sweeping, cherished brushstroke.

The space I have unwittingly created in my clothes closet, between the row of red and row of black garments, tempts me to purchase yet another black sweater. Perhaps I smugly maintain that space for spontaneity or for adding one more frivolous piece to my wardrobe, proving that I am not rigid, that I will someday cull that limp old black blazer that served me well. Content not to be seeking
a replacement for it.

I find comfort in my spaces: the wall in the back bedroom where, at this time, no picture hangs, the empty side of one of my dresser drawers, and the foyer closet with plenty of room
for a loved one's coat and hat on a wintry day.

The Winters of Life

I never knew it was winter until springtime arrived. What is winter but a pure white blanket of snow under which I snuggle to bolster my fortitude and test my mettle? The weight of sunless days rests on my shoulders and sinks into the depths of my soul revealing the light of my secret joys and inner strength. Recognition of a winter storm subdued comes only when I feel the wellspring of hope and promise of spring wash over me and I bask in the warmth of continuance. Late in the year when evening breezes blow cool across my face, like my cat, my coat thickens and I do not shiver beneath the winter cold.

"Prowling his own backyard or asleep by the fire, he is still only a whisker away from the wilds." —Jean Burden (1914-2008)

Contentment

My cat and I went out to sit on the deck
and enjoy a cool, but sunshiny day.
Book and glass of wine in hand,
I didn't even sit down.
True the January sun shone brightly,
but it belied the chill in the air.
So I reluctantly went back inside,
and my cat, KittySweet, followed me.

Settling at my kitchen table to read,
I was forced to contend with my cat's
rubbing his whiskered face against the
corners of the pages of my book.
Stubborn cat, refusing to relax and settle
for sunshine through the window.
Attempting to soothe and oblige
his restless spirit, I picked up his brush
and began to move the bristles along
the length of his back. He opened
his mouth wide and benignly wrapped
his fierce looking teeth around my sweater
covered arm. I put the brush aside.
With my hand, I began stroking his coat,
which sparkled beneath the rays of the sun.
He hunkered down in repose.
Resigned to his fate.

I understand how that feels. *No worries,*
I say to him. Spring will come. Chipmunks
and moles will tease. Sun will warm your
shoulders. The hunt will begin afresh.
Can I expect the return of spring vitality?
Maybe not. I am in limbo now.
In the autumn of my years.
Sunshine through the window is enough.
The touch of a hand is good but not necessary.
A telephone call from a son, a message from
a friend is quite satisfactory for me now,
as well as the soft purr of my contented cat.

Funeral in My Home Town

Regretfully, we sometimes learn who people are by listening to their eulogies. Hearing the pastor speak of my best friend's brother, I was introduced to a man I hardly knew, a sensitive, loving, and talented individual whom I wished I could have known better. We grew up in the same small town. How little I knew of our commonality. I left the funeral home pondering the grinding reality of human value and the beauty and uniqueness of individual stories. None is insignificant.

Driving slowly, I found myself captivated by the familiar houses and businesses, realizing that in my youth nothing was important except my destination when I walked the streets of this small town, hundreds of times. The house I grew up in is no longer there, having been replaced by a large grocery store and parking lot. All lined up on this street, at intervals, are the funeral home, the YMCA building where I spent hours at the movies, swimming pool and teenage canteen, the homes of some of my friends, the First Baptist Church, and the former homes of my two husbands.

On that afternoon I saw these places with a
sense of reverence. I remembered the people
who were sitting on their porches years ago
when I strolled by without acknowledging their
existence. Continuing my drive, I passed the
high school I attended and felt the rush of the
happy memories of my time there. The building
appeared to be standing nobly, attesting to the
validity of each person who has passed through
its halls, some of whom I carelessly ignored
in my teenage exclusivity.

As I drove out of the town limits, I felt
a strong connection to the people I knew least in
my childhood. I regretted that I had not waved to
the textile mill workers and their families sitting on
their porch rockers as I walked down the sidewalk
in front of their homes, or learned their names or
heard their stories. I wished I could return to my
senior classroom, widen my circle and ask them all
to sign my yearbook and be my friends.

Free Walking

Have you ever watched a leashed dog
alongside his master who is not quite in step
with him? Every now and then the dog will begin
loping along trying to catch the rhythm of his
partner, only to find himself lagging behind.
Then he'll break into a trot, overtake the old guy
and turn around and give him a bewildered look.

Have you ever felt like this dog?
Idling, lurching, spinning around to get your
bearings? I have. That's why I walk alone.
I am an old dog and require an even pace.
That way the jumbled pieces of my life can stay
in the spaces for which they were shaped.
I have figured out where I am going,
not necessarily how long it will take to get there.

Yes, I know, walking with someone is pleasant,
and I love to talk…and I have forbearing friends
who kindly give me the opportunity to do so.
But the walk itself is the experience, to be
mentally, physically wrung out and savored.
How blessed to do this without stepping to an
ill-fitted pace! Happy are the times I share with
people. But I must walk unfettered through life,
cherishing the love of friends and family.
No tether to constrain me.

When to Get Off the Codger-Crowded Dance Floor

Space is needed on the dance floor for the younger versions of yourself. They have seen what you have. If not, they have certainly heard about it. When you find yourself holding onto your wine glass longer than your partner, it is time to sit back and watch the show. You are not the only one who knows how to make the right moves and throw parties and get invited to the best ones in town.

When you frequently carry some of the hors d'oeuvres home with you on the front of your outfit, you realize there is a youthful art to standing around a table, gracefully laughing, chatting and devouring a plate of food with no appearance that eating had anything to do with the activity.

When your neighbors call you ma'am and clerks at the store call you honey, when you are the oldest person at the meeting and the first to arrive, you know that the dance belongs to them. And this is good. You watch and enjoy and applaud your own memories and listen to the lilt of the music that lingers in your mind. You mingle with the dancers as long as you can, even though you have wistfully ceded the spotlight.

Don't Forget to Look in the Mirror

What if that wild hair is pushing out of your chin again? What if someone sees it?
Will they know any more about you than they already did? No. It is but another reminder that we are all the same, capable of producing something different, taking on a comedic new shape or slithering out of our old skin
every now and then.

What if we take these pesky little creations of ours a little more seriously? The one that appears on the middle of my chin is usually quite rigid and snow white and demands a couple of tweezer yanks before it realizes its insignificance and lets go. But it will be back.

The light brown hair that grows just above my left jawbone is always fluffy and curly and makes me laugh at the end of the day when I realize that it has been flapping away for hours, enjoying its anonymity and enduring my idle chatter. I almost dislike plucking it away. I await its mischievous return.

I have little control over the black emergence that squeezes out of the crease of my smile just above the expressive corner of my lip. I angrily attack it with my razor, because it is dark and ugly and wickedly warns me not to forget to look in the mirror.

When the novelty wore off…..

A thump on the morning paper in front
of his face stopped leading to a playful jaunt
together down the hallway.

My stories after an afternoon of bridge with my
friends lost all relevance and elicited
only a telling sigh.

Not even a delightfully successful dinner party,
with stimulating conversation among perfect
guests, could draw a response to my humorous
critiques as we cleared the table together.

When the novelty wore off, and it took years, the
realization that it was just a game anyway startled
me. I had been the real me all along, and he had
been the puppeteer, I his marionette.

After the novelty wears off, real people go
on being happy, left to be themselves, content to
be alone. What happens to the gamesplayer, the
puppeteer?

The Eyes Have It

Waiting for the slightest hint of amusement
on my face, his mischievous eyes challenge me
to laugh at his naughty antic. I dare not flinch
lest it be taken as approval and met with peals
of laughter that Granny has capitulated.
Oh, those expressive brown eyes that allow
me to see the heart of my dear grandson!
They revealed his wonder at the tender feelings
he had for his cat, Mufasa. They sparkled with
the-world-is-mine joy of sitting in his first car
on his sixteenth birthday. They were warm and
loving his freshman year in college when, home
for the holidays, he smiled and said "Merry
Christmas, Granny!" They were the confident
and proud eyes of a college grad smoothly
moving through the family activities on the day
of his younger brother's graduation from his alma
mater. Oh, those expressive brown eyes of my
dear grandson, Will, still full of mischief, love,
joy and confidence!

Connections

My nightly prayers are short, my morning prayers long, when I reach deeply into my soul and connect with the inner peace that slows my step and sets straight my path for the day.
I am in my sanctuary. Seated at my kitchen table, gathering my thoughts and materials for my morning meditation, I pause and glance through the corner window.
There he is; I knew he would be.

The patriarch of the squirrel community in my section of the neighborhood often balances himself between the bottom branch and crooked trunk of the tree by my kitchen window. He is as big as a cat and his tail seems to stay bushy all summer. When he looks my way, his gaze is steady and intentional, seemingly expressing an understanding of our commonality.

I wonder where squirrels go when it is time for them to die, that is, if they have escaped the ire of human predators who begrudge their taking a small share of the bird seed. Or, I wonder if he will miss me when I no longer occupy my seat at the kitchen table at sunrise.

Umbrellas

Young women, young mothers I should say, in the
absence of feathered wings, create umbrellas.
Beneath these amazing gadgets they dwell, along
with the fledglings they have birthed. No
bombardments or pouring on of life's perplexities
penetrate this resistance against happenstance.
With great agility and swiftness of foot, these
young mothers circumvent sinkholes.
Their strong arms and stronger instincts hoist these
domes above their charges and at the end of the
day settle them into readiness.

One by one the fledglings find their soulmates,
create their own umbrellas and drift away. They
look backward to the cherished days of ease and,
if they are discerning, discover the source of their
resolution. Perchance when they are tempted to
retreat to this haven, if it remains, and relax into its
comfort, they find a loving soul still standing,
alone and awash in the infirmities
seeping through the tattered dome above her.

Old Woman and Cat

Neither desires any longer
 to capture
and devour the prey that
once lured them to
suddenly lunge and snatch
and conquer.

It is good to sit and gaze
from the window at the
pitiable ones still in search
of purpose
and relevance.

One sighs, the other purrs,
and both blend
into the landscape
to which they belong.

*"In ancient times cats were worshipped;
they have not forgotten this."*
—*Terry Pratchett (1948-2015)*

Annual Christmas Party

Here
we are again
clustered in a room
together, sighing and
pretending to be casting
bored looks at one another
when we wouldn't have missed
being here for anything even if it
meant ditching our walkers behind
shrubbery at the entrance or having
to sit by the same persons we did last
year hearing the same tired stories and
hoping the food would be lavish and the
entertainment minimal and that our wine
glasses will remain in the upright position
as well as our bodies in
hopes of
returning
next year.

My Trusting Heart

My trusting heart relinquished its vigilance for the warmth of perceived certainty. Nestled in the sunshine, it had no thought of an impending cloud that could obscure its comfort or shift its foundation. By the time my heart noticed the cracks beneath us, I had smoothed them away with one fleet swipe of my right foot; my left foot was headed toward tomorrow.

Musings

How insignificant the kind of love
that thrives on the strength of its
object and abhors the whimpering
of the weary soul when it stumbles.

I Want to Go Back
To Lauren on Her High School Graduation
From her Granny

Here you are on the brink of young womanhood,
and I am still spinning from the gathering speed of
the emergence of a lovely young teenager, gently,
yet swiftly moving through her childhood years.
Even as those cherished years were unfolding
I was clinging to them, knowing how significant
they were, will always be, to my personal journey.

Now I want to go back there. I want to coax you
into revisiting all the magical moments we shared,
ask you to listen to my memories, recapture them
in your heart and make them stay alive for me! I
want you to feel my joy in looking upon a little,
upturned face that without words eagerly cried out
"Granny, what are we going to do today?"

When you and I were together, everything became
an event, and the events flowed without plans. I
want to once again open our "bag of tricks" and
explore its contents with all the enthusiasm that
beset us time and time again as we spread about us
an indescribable array of sequins, lace, felt,

sparkling beads, scraps of cloth and whatever trinkets I had tucked away over the years.
I want to see once more the happy contentment settle on your sweet face as your little fingers sew, glue and create memories for your Granny.

Back to an open field I want to fly with you and pick wildflowers for a bouquet. To a woodsy spot I want us to retreat and find our make-believe house in Narnia and the remnants of our prior "decorations." I want to come home and find on my front porch a rock that you have left for me, one that you considered just right for your Granny. I want to find more red and yellow mushrooms, even if we must fend off fire ants. A long walk I want to take with you and hear your precocious thoughts about family, God and friendships.

Again I want to wear your mother's old prom dress and be Princess Lauren's lady-in-waiting, with Will and Jack in tow. I want to go through my drawers and cover you with glitzy clothes and jewelry and find an evening bag and high heeled shoes for you and watch you parade about the house.

I want to see you all dressed up in your dance costume with cheeks painted and hair curled as you execute the dance recital steps with tiny fingers moving gracefully through the air. I want to wake up on a Saturday morning and, along with my two cats, see this beautiful child, you, Lauren, whose head rests on the pillow beside me.

But we cannot go back, and it is not necessary. All these memories and many, many more linger in my heart and mind and are refreshed every time I see your sweet, smiling face. So spin and laugh and dance and enjoy all that life can offer, dear granddaughter, but keep this little girl forever in your spirit.

www.ingramcontent.com/pod-product-compliance
Lightning Source LLC
Chambersburg PA
CBHW072103290426
44110CB00014B/1804